DISCARD

Woodbourne Library
Washington-Centerville Public Lib.
Centerville, Ohio

W9-CLV-042

I Love Sports

Swimming

by Allan Morey

Bullfrog Books

Ideas for Parents and Teachers

Bullfrog Books let children practice reading informational text at the earliest reading levels. Repetition, familiar words, and photo labels support early readers.

Before Reading

- Discuss the cover photo. What does it tell them?

- Look at the picture glossary together. Read and discuss the words.

Read the Book

- "Walk" through the book and look at the photos. Let the child ask questions. Point out the photo labels.

- Read the book to the child, or have him or her read independently.

After Reading

- Prompt the child to think more. Ask: Have you been in a swimming race? Have you watched a swimming meet? Did you notice anything different about the pool?

Bullfrog Books are published by Jump!
5357 Penn Avenue South
Minneapolis, MN 55419
www.jumplibrary.com

Copyright © 2015 Jump! International copyright reserved in all countries. No part of this book may be reproduced in any form without written permission from the publisher.

Library of Congress Cataloging-in-Publication Data

Morey, Allan.
 Swimming / by Allan Morey.
   pages cm. — (I love sports)
Summary: "This photo-illustrated book for early readers introduces the basics of swimming and encourages kids to try it. Includes labeled diagram of swimming pool and photo glossary." — Provided by publisher
 Includes index.
 Audience: Age: 5.
 Audience: Grade: K to Grade 3.
 ISBN 978-1-62031-182-0 (hardcover) —
 ISBN 978-1-62496-269-1 (ebook)
1. Swimming for children — Juvenile literature. I. Title.
 GV837.2.H64 2015
 797.2'1—dc23

                                    2014032131

Series Editor: Rebecca Glaser
Series Designer: Ellen Huber
Book Designer: Anna Peterson
Photo Researcher: Jenny Fretland VanVoorst

Photo Credits: All photos by Shutterstock except: Corbis, 6–7, 23br; Dreamstime, 12–13, 22, 23ml; Getty, 3, 18, 20–21; Thinkstock, 5, 8, 16–17, 23tl.

Printed in the United States of America at Corporate Graphics in North Mankato, Minnesota.

Table of Contents

Let's Swim!

Put on your swimsuit.

**Jump in the water.
Let's swim!**

5

There is a meet today.
Kids go to the pool.
They will race.

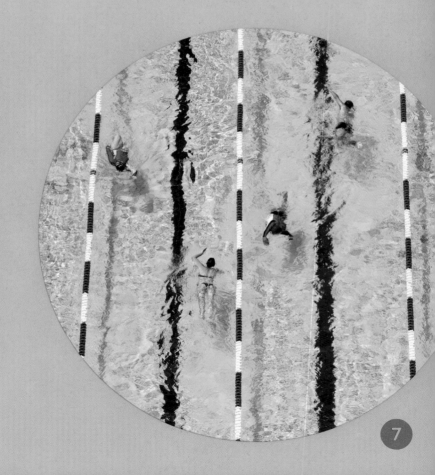

Sam gets ready.

The whistle blows.
Tweet!

The race starts.

The swimmers dive in.

Splash!

lap · · · · ·▶

One length of the pool is a lap.

Some races are one lap.

Some are many laps.

Ali does the front crawl.
Her arms reach forward.
She kicks her legs.

Amir is on his back.

He does the backstroke.

He swings his arms
over his head.

Mia was
the fastest.

18

She won her race.

She gets a medal.

Do you want to try?

Dive in.

Swimming is fun!

At a Swim Meet

lane marking

lane line

lane

starting block

Picture Glossary

backstroke
When you swim on your back and swing your arms backward.

lap
One length of the swimming pool is a lap.

dive
To jump into the water head first.

medal
An award for doing well.

front crawl
Swimming by reaching forward with one arm at a time to pull yourself through the water.

meet
An event where many swimmers compete in different races.

23

Index

To Learn More

Learning more is as easy as 1, 2, 3.

1) Go to www.factsurfer.com

2) Enter "swimming" into the search box.

3) Click the "Surf" button to see a list of websites.

With factsurfer.com, finding more information is just a click away.